DUSK

OTHER BOOKS BY MATTHEW BARTON

Learning to Row, Peterloo 1999
Vessel, Brodie Press 2009
Family Tree, Shoestring Press, 2016
Duino Elegies (R.M. Rilke), Shoestring Press 2019

DUSK

MATTHEW BARTON

Shoestring Press

Printed by imprintdigital
Upton Pyne, Exeter
www.digital.imprint.co.uk

Typesetting and cover design by The Book Typesetters
us@thebooktypesetters.com
07422 598 168
www.thebooktypesetters.com

Published by Shoestring Press
19 Devonshire Avenue, Beeston, Nottingham, NG9 1BS
(0115) 925 1827
www.shoestringpress.co.uk

First published 2021
© Copyright: Matthew Barton
© Cover painting: Francesca Goodrich-Barton

The moral right of the author has been asserted.

ISBN 978-1-912524-75-4

ACKNOWLEDGEMENTS

'Chapel of Rest' won the 2018 Strokestown poetry competition. 'Whitsun', and a version of 'Walking the Frome' were first published in *Paintings & Poems: In Conversation*, privately published 2019. 'Walking the Frome' also appeared in *Scintilla* 21. 'Trespass' appeared in *Strike Up the Band: Poems for John Lucas at 80,* Plas Gwyn Books 2017. 'My Dead' appeared in *Raceme* magazine.

I am indebted to an Authors' Foundation grant from the Society of Authors, which was very helpful in completing this book. Thanks to Sue Booth-Forbes and all at Anam Cara, Ireland, for a wonderfully restorative stay. Thanks as ever to Philip Lyons, David Cook and David Whitwell for their suggestions and support. Thanks to Tim and Melanie for the caravan.

CONTENTS

DUSK

Clouds upon clouds – the horizon
above the hill was a cloud-theatre's various
depths of scenery, shapes
of softer and darker grey, all shifting
across the whole grey backdrop.

And a racket up on the hill:
some big tractor or other machinery
grinding away, its headlights like the glow
of a welder's torch in the gloom.
It was rumbling on, juddering and whining
when out of the cloud world perhaps –
another world surely – a great white owl

came ghosting over the treetops,
sails of its wings sensing
the depths of the overgrown field beneath.
It was a spirit if ever I saw one:
ominous, serene. It was death
bearing the world alive
through living dark.

MY DEAD

Sometimes it seems my dead
are looking into the back of my mind
and see the world that way:
the far side of the brain where I
have not yet closed myself
a priest-hole place – where what is vaster, uglier
lives its deep-sea creature life.

That's where they congregate.

The pretty thoughts I send them hardly touch
their vivid flux –
so inchoate they are, so far adrift
from who I think they were.
They're growing ever otherward,
their silence in me just my own deaf ear
to their intimate oracle.

GRAVE

It is said that when small
I outlined my baby brother on the floor
with buttons, in a pattern
enclosing him.

Sixty years on
I'm placing sea-smoothed stones and shells
around his headstone,
planting cyclamen

and see I am doing this again.
He never would conform:
too angry and alive back then and since
too dead and gone.

Thomas, all these years
I was shaping my life around
the brilliance, fury, first, and then
the loss of you.

I hope you agree it's time
I let you get on with your death at last,
put myself
into the empty space you left

in me.
It's mine.

KITTENS

Why should your son drown,
the kittens live?
They didn't.
You handed me
the bucket's weight.

Perhaps you said nothing
but I knew what needed doing.
I took it like the man
I was not nearly yet but this
might hold me to being – carried it swilling
and slopping off balance out

to the heath, not looking tipped
weak thumps into a bush.
Returned, not yet
wondering why I had to be
complicit in this act. Not yet
getting it: the grief that keeps

coming up for air however much
you hold it down and wait for it to stop.

ADVICE

The newborn dead
generally latch on quick
to the lacrimal gland
and suck.

It is a little known fact
that tears are nutritious for them,
strengthening their sense
of having lived.

This gets them off to a good start.
Don't worry if you find they feed
at irregular hours and even if
you wake up weeping in the night.

This sap
creates a bond with you which will
stand them in good stead. Although
you might occasionally feel depleted by

their unrelenting thirst for you,
remember they are new to this
and not yet ready to give up
the sweet and sudden flow of grief.

IT WAS ONLY THE WIND

but the way it twisted
the window off, lifted it as if
with both hands, let it drop and smash –
the satisfactory
rending of wood,
the microtonal squeal
of snapping glass – reminded me
of all your breakages, the way the pure
hell of them would rip up
silence to make space you thought perhaps
for something in us more alive.

Compulsively before your glare I'd sweep
the pieces into a pile and shovel them
into the bin. But not today.

I revelled in the shock. I almost missed
your furies for a second. Pitied us.
And in your memory I let them lie:

the mess of splinters, bits of fallen sky.

HEART ATTACK

It couldn't go on
but it did:
the fury flowering in you
at me,
my seething withdrawal,
the window of speech stuck
shut then shattering
between us, bitten lips.

We couldn't go on:
those rages in the long
reach of the night,
me pressing all my weight
against the door
to stop you
breaking through

to me, me quite honestly
wanting to stop your mouth.
No giving no forgiving:
something had to give.

Is there a law that what seems strongest
hides the weakest place?

Too strong, too much for me.
But you gave out.

GOOD NIGHT

No idea you would die.
But in the last few days
a gentleness:

patience, a sense
you wanted to know me
differently. No anger.

I felt it but couldn't
bring myself there.
The last evening

you came down – it seems now in farewell –
to sit at the table.
So vivid my turning to go

to my bed and my brief
Good night then. Not knowing
that was my last chance to speak

words different, deeper and kinder.

CHAPEL OF REST

It didn't much matter at the end of the day
that the clothes I'd sent for you,
blue velvet and red,
were buttoned a shade or two tight.

Though if I'd taken the trouble
to look more carefully I might have known
you'd not worn those things
for ages now, but kept them as
remembrance: old flames in the dark.

I sat there quite a while.
And then got up, undid
the buttons, as if
to let you breathe a bit.

It didn't much matter that another had dressed you
for the first time since you were young.
Your grandmother might have done it: one-handed,
a little carelessly.

I couldn't undo the wrong.

ASHES

Heavier than I thought,
about the weight
of a late miscarriage.

The haul of you I bear to the car.

And drive oh so carefully, suddenly
remembering how I drove you

home from the hospital holding
our newborn daughter:

putting the softest brakes on,
easing them off with a prayer.

IN CAMERA

As one carries the living world into a sickroom
in flowers, say, or grapes,
from time to time I bring
some small thing to mind for you. Today
your oldest and youngest grandsons –
see how beautiful each.

The room in my mind
I make for you may be
small but do
look in if you will:

the oldest, lithe suddenly, on the swivel
where self begins to tread
a deepening weight
but bearing it like a prince
with a smile wrung
almost unwillingly from him.

And the youngest one rush
of want and delight.

Here, sip this. I believe I can see you
developing these glimpses
into a life that's full beyond my reach.

LIMINAL

Here's chocolate
and croissants waxed
with sweal of butter,
blackberries picked
before the devil spat: now feast

on loss at least with us.
The table's laid: dear shade
who was my wife,
be welcome, help us eat away
the night.

Don't you remember? Here
beside us is your place.

SABRE WASP

For Francesca

Do you miss her too?
It was hard to answer.
I wanted to tell you I did
but I do and I don't.

And at that moment flitting
on the windowsill between
fragments of her etched,
her luminous glass:
a narrow-waisted,
silver-winged insect trailing
a stinger's line and hook.

Trapped in a jar she fluttered danger.
Carried to the door I shook her out
and she juddered into flight.

Those terrible battles. We belonged
to each other like the wound
in ourselves we refused to accept.

Not a stinger at all, I discovered,
but an *ovipositor* to stitch
eggs into grubs deep in wood:
death to her offspring's host
yet for all that still
vulnerable, beautiful.

RUNNING ON EMPTY

Surprising how long I have kept on
going on nothing.
A year since you died.
It's not that I think things would have got better between us.
No, I don't believe that.

But the life I thought I wanted without you –
after all empty when given me
without a fight.

The truth is we gave each other
more than we knew:
a spark continually reigniting
the hurt that before it killed you
kept refuelling our life.

Did you take it with you – the spell
to heal the heart?
You know the old tale:
the shadow from a splinter of the blade that made
the wound, when it's held
up to the light.

Now where do I find that?

ANAM CARA

Take the path that winds
its ferns through the wood,
descend to a clearing, stand
dumbstruck at the thunder
of the river carving itself
a passage to hold its own
molten plunge, its trumpet blast
and cannonade through rock.

Wander further, cross
a bridge and come
to where the river sweeps
its soft and cooling charge.

Sit there under hazel: everything
has stopped at last. The quiet

could make you weep.

SONG

The woman taken in adultery. John 8, 6–11

Why that moment speaks to me
more than anything: when urged
to come down on one side, instead
of falling for the wordtrap he will not
reply
but writes
an indecipherable sign in dust
as if his finger tells the pulse

of earth, of all we've done, the wrong
that belongs to everyone

as if it touches in to the silence
under every sentence:
the truth that being
of one body what can we do but try
to mend each other in the end.

RAPHAEL'S DRAWINGS

We agreed that seeing the first
self-portrait would have done:
we could have stood there a long time, then left
with more than enough:
the eyes especially, the look
of knowing ancient as the sun in the soft
dawn of his face.

But we walked dutifully around, almost
unwillingly wondering at the way
muscles and drapery and flesh
kept breaking into life, and somehow
grasping less and less:

how he could capture
truth in the turn of a neck,
the slant of a wrist, the ripeness
of a lip. I tried saying something to you
about him not copying
but creating the world. But words
fell flat. Instead

I kept wanting to lean
in to you and know
the delicate suffering of your skin, the intimate
bones of content.

EXAMINATION

On my side with knees up
in the recovery position, am I
doing penance for some
deep transgression on a day
– of all days – of collision
between the first of Lent and Valentine's?

One finger up to my prostate
and prodding, I wonder if the physician
tires of this procedure, and if he's thinking,
this grey mid-week, of other things
he might be doing. Over in no time and

pants up I'm reinstated
upon a chair in a dignified position.
But however we choose not to dwell
precisely on what has passed between us
and though he will hand me on

to the nurse without so much
as a goodbye – for he's a busy man –
it has, hasn't it, and the intimacy
of touching there
seems, though well-sunk
in the proper formality, something

making us both for a moment
sorry and more loving.

HIDDEN

Hungry Hill, Beara

From the road it rears over you
Lofty rockhead in the cloud,
blind face.

Start to climb it opens to admit you: swards
of green between the stone ridges
so you find yourself zig-zagging up
the stations of ascent.
And when the terraces end
there are footholds of heather and gorse.
The mountain seems to want
to give you a leg up – to spread
its far visions at your feet.

But going over behind
the backdrop, stumbling around shiftless
boulders, descending
to the hidden lake, you find
mountain's great shrine to itself:
sheer plummet of rock
into its black reflection.

Then suddenly you're fearful in this place
where you're not meant to be
and your life after all
is so tiny in depth.

MASS ROCK
Beara

Today only the sea
is a hushed congregation.
God himself his own lonely
altar and priest, a ghost

hanging over this place.
Great slabs vault above
the long flat kneeling rock:
to kneel into the hard

mountain, to cleave
to the barren life
that was their lot – what faith:
enough to make an obdurate

god exist,
to lure him like
invoking smoke then flicker
from sodden turf.

COAST PATH

I looked down from above
on the kestrel's back,
its one held note.

The sea was tearing itself to shreds.
The kestrel did not even
flutter in the rush
of wind, it was still as belief.

Such a lonely existence I thought,
the bird lifted and stopped there and holding
its own against spray and gust.

But I was thinking of course of my self
stopped there looking down

not the bird knowing only
the greater self of the wind
with never beginning or end

OLD HAWK

As I was about to head downhill
a hawk sailed over the trees,
wings stretched before the sun –
which showed him to be a tattered bird,
flight-feathers missing like the many
lost teeth of a comb.

Threadbare but nevertheless
he circled and hovered with the grace
of an old pro, unfurled
the battle-torn flag of himself: hung there,
was gone before I knew.

BIRDSONG AT RHYDWILYM

A natural clock not so much measuring
time as making it
in a myriad clicking

catches and quivering springs,
these intricacies that clink against
each other collide then strike

astonished harmony together:
each tiny well is pulsing its
fresh reel or sometimes simply

a sweet insisting pressure on the ear.

I know I'll never learn but still
I'm listening…

antiphonal alarms
spell in this now that never has
that's always been before

not minutes and seconds those blunt bells
but all the trembling scales of being

ever differently attuned and all the more
alive precisely since so only

momentarily

PIPISTRELLES

Folded all day like the stash
of letters in an escritoire,
do they forget what they meant?

Till dusk unlocks the lid,
draws out each tremble of parchment to flutter
their quivery script before her failing sight, to press them

to her ancient breast.

A SPELL FOR ASH

Black nails of ash, bare finger-bones –
oh dry wishbone put on your dress
of feather-leaf, be aureole again,
be sun-creel. Queen of sylphs put on
your shift of lace, and flash
the gleam and mysteries of matter
shivering into light.
Fairy-fingered dancer, throw your net
of fresh shadows at our feet.
Not these dead knuckles.
Still be kaleidoscope of green,
an oracle of grace.

ELM

For Tim

Not dead but in limbo
you said. The saplings

shoot from the bole with an eye
to the main chance,

get knee-high but then
are riddled with beetle-shot again.

Cloned poles they stand memorial
to immaturity. Not dead

but stopped, knocked back,
yet still compulsively

hoisting little flags to show
their no surrender even though

it's not clear how this differs from defeat.

PRUNUS

is a thorn in my neighbours' side,
sending its scions
under the boundary, springing up

like a quiver of rude jokes among
their roses and hydrangeas.
They regard me as if I'm whispering it

secret encouragement: why don't I rein it in,
chop it back or even hack it down and drill
a hole in the stump and pour in poison?

It's not only the slender phalli
causing offence but the fact
that its crown is becoming a clamouring

crowd at their toilet window
and before long will be tangling
with the overstrung power cable.

Yes, I will prune it, I say, knowing
that will send it shooting from the hip.
I might remind them how it flickers

into flower in earliest spring,
its trusty old standard holding
a mothlight to the gloom.

Or I might tell them how my daughter
when young once opened the front door after rain
and sat on the step listening

to its blackbird's song.

FALL
R. M. Rilke

Leaves come tumbling, flocking as from far
withering gardens in the sky, their fall
flutters resignation in the air.
And earth each night is lapsing from the whole
firmament of the stars into its lone
and sundered weight. This falling's going on
in all of us, it pulls upon my arm.
And yet there stands
in the midst of this falling one who holds it all
in utterly tranquil hands.

FALL

For Melanie & Tim

Is it true a leaf
falls to make space
for next year's bud
that swelling ousts it
from its little plinth?

If so then we who leap here in this wood
to catch careering leaves mid-air
you say it means good luck to catch
are leaves ourselves the earth's new crop
of hope is slowly pushing off the edge.
And who will catch us?
God, wrote Rilke, holds all falling in
an infinite palm; but say it's down to us

to know ourselves in freefall, catch
momentarily alight – as we do laughing,
leaping here for crazy life. The leaves

seem bent on eluding our clutch. We dive
headlong but they skedaddle out of reach.
As if their only freedom lay in this
frolic, in their sly last gasp
evasion of our grasp.

TRESPASS

Cars rush by us
on the A46
but over the stone stile
is like entering
a sound-proofed room:
a rich man's estate
of landscaped slopes, idyllic oaks.

An elegant outdoor drawing room,
silence broken only by the odd
pheasant's starter-motor cough as it
nearly rattles itself apart
before careering off.

Some way below us a jeep
slows to a stop to check
who we think we are
then roars away to report.

There are sheep. There's a trip-wired field
of fodder maize, signs to keep out.

But over the next brow a man
who probably comes from that very different kind
of estate whose dishes and roofs you see
in the distance, is harvesting
with the latter-day scythe he got for a song:
he's foraging
for whatever turns up.
What's turned up –

he shows us with pleasure –
is a Roman nail. Head like a helmet,
long square shank.

I'm wondering if they crucified people here.

And we turn together, the man and us
and gaze across
to Gurney's Severn and those hills of his.

WALKING THE FROME

For Rachel and in memory of Carter

By Snuff Mills you're extinguished
to slug brown, girding your loin
for the cover-up coming, the decline
below tarmac, slow trudge
through the gut of the city.

But you flicker into life as I follow you out
past Frenchay and under the shudder
of a ring road through bramble and copse, across fields:
not quite singing but starting to whisper
of things once being livelier –

weary of the future but as yet
not oblivious of beginnings. Round bends
you show flare on occasion, refusal
to think yet of culverts waiting
to siphon and swallow you
though some might detect subtle darkening
of mood in your chatter.

Near Frampton Cotterell you're humming
in the mouths of stone bridges,
shrugging your way past old workings
at Iron Acton and cutting your losses
in fields where you might be mistaken

for glorified ditches. You keep flowing,
at moments a leash quivering on
the tug of bad portents, at others
remembering the spring you unspool from
you let down your hair in a clear
torrent of abandon.

It's at Yate though when you've been yet again
artificially channelled and straitened
and are clogged up with tatters of plastic,
rusty tins and thick gunk
that you're suddenly emblazoned
in a white heron sailing serene
from your tongue like the soul
having done with it all and ascending.

WALKING

Is this actually the right path?
All those hesitancies and

anxieties: all those tiny
arrhythmias of intent.

I lift off from full
trust in the ground and my feet

hurt, a blister
is starting to bloom. The pain

a sharp master reminding me
what I neglect:

being anywhere other than here.
At each step I fend off

the future or try
to grasp it too fast. I think

of a brook that accepts every hindrance,
flowing through, finding

its way with each pulse.
If only my head stopped trying to hinder

my feet from doing the thinking, perhaps
I'd be here at last and alive to the earth.

FLUENT
For Oscar

Writing, he clings
to the sheer face of the page,
scarcely dare move in the tight
knot of the script.

But on ice, look – he flies
backward, reels round
the spurt of a curve before catching
up with himself for a moment
but only to crack
the whip of the line again, leaning a shoulder
into the speed that he is, shrugging off
all that could cramp or hold him back.

WATER TO WINE

is no miracle.
The grapes do it every year:
each rounds to a wineskin
like a woman conceiving a son,
it happens all the time.

She turned to him, said, *They have no wine.*

A child is of you but not yours –
makes you see
you were only a vessel for something
you could not imagine would come to be.

Do whatever he asks, she said,
knowing it was all beyond her but simply
trusting the space life fills

with its ordinary miracles.

FERMENT

For Francesca

After an argument about the house
as we drive to your mother's grave, we find
a late-flowering elder in the churchyard,
together pick its frothing knots of bloom
and pocket them in a child's cardigan.

The home your life sprang from a tangle
she left you to solve: the lift
and plummet of atmospheres you could not fathom
yet made
the undershade of your self-ownership.

The argument flares again, then days of silence.
I soak the flowers in water that grows thick
with fragrance, when I heave them out
of the bowl the liquid fizzes in my fingers.

Sugar and lemons: sweetness and bitterness both
belong in the mix.
Bottled, it seethes.

Here is your share: although
I'd spare you all the bother if I could,
I could not spare you then.
You want to own it. Must.
So every day unstopper
these thunder-flasks to vent themselves then quickly
cork them before they erupt.

We each do this religiously, learn how
to let them speak but not

spew all their riches out.

Daily they're subdued. You tell me
you've taught them who's in charge.

Now when we free
the harness from their throats they speak
at last more softly, gradually subsiding
to a sprinkling whisper, hush.

DAISY BRAZIER-LE-MUIR

Thanks for lending me twenty-five quid,
– two crisp notes –
in a bus when all I had
was small change that kept changing
in my dream, sometimes more, sometimes less
but however I counted it never
quite enough.

Yours was the human face.
You were just getting off
and I had to insist
you give me your name for repayment.
I took great pains to repeat
and repeat it. On waking I still had it right
though the look of your face

had gone out apart from the glimmer
of a general kindness – which,
though I looked you up to find
you do not exist,

persists.

BINSEY CHURCH

Truss of ancient timbers,
pews are so many rows
of ship's seats facing forward
assuredly to the future.
Here I attend
to the sermon of breeze, the slanting floor
of souls long underfoot.
Oil lamps out, but someone has lit the flickering
North Star of a taper on the altar.

In earshot time is thundering off
on the dual carriageway, leaving this place
adrift in its own quiet:
the comfort of a simple destination once
everyone more or less was making for.
People come and sit here, muse awhile
in this hold of half-light vaguely perhaps
recalling promises which, though never quite
kept, cannot finally be dispelled

then pull themselves together, go outside,
fade into their lives.

MIRROR

What's up, what's down? In icy flood,
trees' winter brushwork, mist-shorn sun,
the swerve of birds that lift
deeper in their mirroring
like something perfectly intact.

And coming from the water's face
a child carries in two hands
– an open book? illumined screen?
She gazes at its script of stars
as if she read her wholeness there.

She bears it like an altar tray. She brings it
to her father who kindly bends
to receive this pure device

as if her offering is a piece
of the silence any utterance will break.

STROKE

Suddenly words no longer get in the way.
You beam at me simply
happy I'm here.
There's little to be said, leastways
little you can say. Who cares
about words anyway? As if the whole
face of a cliff fell off
a high peak, revealed

another face shining beneath.
You're still smiling though words come out
jumbled. It's almost a joke,
this speaking of words or being not
able to speak them.

I'm strangely happy with you in a way
I'm not sure I remember. Always
words my stumbling blocks (that did not
come clear in my mouth
as yours did, silver-quick and brightly judged
like coins I never could pay back
in the same swift currency,
that sense
of being slow off the mark).

And this is the game we play now:
you laboriously shaping sounds
and smiling while I wait
to make your meaning out, and laughing
with me when I don't.

Both of us released: now meaning's lost
its knife-edge love words got in the way of seems
enough at last.

STRUGGLE

You stutter: *I'm like a four year old.*
Struggling for an hour
to write a note, getting muddled
about which medicine to take,
labouring again and again to say
a word that won't come right
then gritting your teeth
in mock fury (still smiling).

You drum words
of one syllable along
the table top till they all
sort of line up:
a slovenly bunch of recruits.
Words failing you gesture and point.

And always you reach for my hand
not in need but in love.

Some might say this is not
the person you were but I say
the damming of fluency's released
a spring of patience in you: sap
of tenderness that's seeping
beautifully through stricken speech.

LISTENING

Waiting on your
each word that comes
slow as a misshapen leaf
from its laborious bud
and while it pushes its
way into being there is
all the time in the world
to want that word
to form, to welcome it
and help the next be born.

Your words are drops
ripening on a wire
until they acquire the right
weight to fall.

How is it your hand
rests patient in mine?
How come
now it's so hard
for you to speak
we seem to be speaking more easily
than we've ever done?

QUESTION

Are   *you*   *hap*   *py?*
you ask from nowhere.
Yes, I say, *I am.*

Not a question I think
you ever asked me before
in such simplicity

nor an answer
I could ever
before have given so easily.

ORDINARY
For Rachel

I am very ordinary you said.
And suddenly

ordinary was everything I could want:
the sun shining simply,

run-of-the-mill grass, each
uncomplicated tree,
the customary rain beginning

to ring its humdrum tunes,
the plain wonder
of holding your hand

in this accepted way.

RUNNING ON EMPTY II
With thanks to Andy Goldsworthy

Remembrance Sunday and I've forgotten
to fill up and halfway back
the needle's on less than nothing. I have spent
hours with my grandson
wetting and sticking yellow leaves
to a stone in the stream.
His phone forgotten, hands wet, feet muddy,
changing rock into gold.

The car gives a hiccup
and I'm willing it on
when all too obviously the empty tank
stands in for running out of time,
for being taken at any moment
from all I know too late almost I love.

Today life's wrapped me in its brief
present of light. There may be nowhere else
to get to but I beg
to be allowed to keep on going a bit.

FILLING UP

St. Mary's Well, Maenclochog

This caravan on a hillside beside
thickets of hazel, a bank
of hawthorn, bracken and oak.
Open the door – you hear

the river rustling in the valley,
not much else but birdsong, wind's
arboreal orchestra, occasionally
a car in the steep lane. Rain
rattling the roof. No water tap

or electricity, the wealth
of needing less: wood for the stove,
the good of carrying it
from the forest, candle light.

And I've come to fill up
an assortment of canisters
with water that spouts
from a rock in a gap in the hedge.

Straight off the mountain it pours a chill
tongue into my receptacles,
its sing-song into my ears.

I haul the cans up the hill like jugs of gold,
glad of my cache.

What tons of water streaming here
for centuries, its riches flowing away
unharvested. The little I take
unnoticed in the myriad threads
of rivulets that keep this land alive:

a table from which all is fed.

VALEDICTORY
i.m. Jeremy Mulford

I'll speak to you
when I speak to you.
The voice on the message
clear if frail.

I still have it, the owner
of the voice beyond utterance now.
And *Lots of love...* had he said that before?

My provider tells me
it will be deleted in seven days.
A life silenced.
The reality in it –
you know, every tone
and inflection: the *person,*
that sounding through
of all he'd grown gently to be.

I'll speak to you when I speak to you.
You will Jeremy. You do.

WHITSUN
i.m. Carter Nelson

Stepping out I'm elated by this briar with its flames
of yellow rose, a whole spray of them –
not flames quite: more like
the world's finest skin. You chose this time to go –
this riot of supplication,
the horse chestnut
one nunnery of prayer.

I'm not sure I can do without you.
The birds have gone bonkers – that blackbird…
If only I listened I might know
life is all utterance and death
the fuel of all song.

PASSED AWAY

I never used to like the phrase
but when I got the text today,
was struck somehow
not by its dainty navigation
around blank ending, but

the once-loud hoofs
now on the point of clopping out
of earshot leaving the stillness
fuller for having been, and kept
by grace of memory more alive
in us perhaps in absence than by what
they granted in the actual ear.

And then of course I thought of Frost
one summer dawn writing of winter dusk,
and conjuring snow and silence while his blood
would keep on treading its iambic pulse.

NIGHTFALL

For Rachel

Lacing boots again on sore feet, the dark
has fallen while we stopped.
Leaving the odd light behind
we walk the blind lane steering

by trees blacker than night.
Miles to go and hoping
we're on the right track.
You speechless beside me,

weary of the long tramp.
Willing us on I search
the nothing ahead.
There were times in the past I felt

like lying down in a ditch.
But now your hand in trust
in mine is bringing me to believe
in home however bleak the wind,

however long this darkness is.

BEACH AT TWILIGHT

For Rachel

Coming back to your own
footprints in the sand you stepped
carefully into them again.

That they should fit you
perfectly was no surprise. Surprised
you were though by

the solace of them, how they kept
the way you walked, the length of stride,
how they remembered more of you

than you knew: as if the earth
wears us as we walk and shapes
a slipper of our every step, will hold us

to the destiny that can fit
the one alone who is making it.

EPILOGUE

Like knight and lady on the tomb
though armourless and breathing, we
rest here while light rains in and makes
us solid to ourselves awhile, the bones
we'll be for now still sheathed in flesh.
But this peace in me I haven't known
for most of a lifetime seems to be
a faithful promise kept. One made
so long ago it cannot be recalled
but only called to life again: that love
would find us here at last, make room for us before
the darkness comes that we'll survive once more.